CHUCK GIACINTO & BRYCE CONLAN

CLOUD CULTURE

CHRISTIAN LIVING IN THE SOCIAL MEDIA WORLD

SEVEN LEAF PRESS
CHICAGO
WWW.SEVENLEAFPRESS.COM

CLOUD CULTURE™

Copyright © 2012 Bryce Conlan/Chuck Giacinto

All rights reserved. No part of this book may be reproduced or transmitted in any form or by any means without written permission from the author. Any trademarks, service marks, product names or named features are assumed to be the property of their respective owners, and are used only for reference. There is no implied endorsement with regards to this book or it's contents. The views and opinions expressed in this book are solely those of the authors. Scripture quotations marked "NKJV™" are taken from the New King James Version®. Copyright © 1982 by Thomas Nelson, Inc. Used by permission. All rights reserved. Scripture quotations marked (NIV) are taken from the Holy Bible, New International Version®, NIV®. Copyright © 1973, 1978, 1984, 2011 by Biblica, Inc.™ Used by permission of Zondervan. All rights reserved worldwide. . The www.zondervan.com "NIV" and "New International Version" are trademarks registered in the United States Patent and Trademark Office by Biblica, Inc.™. Scripture quotations taken from the New American Standard Bible®, Copyright © 1960, 1962, 1963, 1968, 1971, 1972, 1973, 1975, 1977, 1995 by The Lockman Foundation. Used by permission." (www.Lockman.org). Scripture quotations from *THE MESSAGE*. Copyright © by Eugene H. Peterson 1993, 1994, 1995, 1996, 2000, 2001, 2002. Used by permission of NavPress Publishing Group."

SEVEN LEAF PRESS LLC.
CHICAGO IL, 60608

"Exceptional Christian Literature"

Reach us on the Internet: **www.SevenLeafPress.com**

ISBN-13: 978-0615650562

ISBN-10: 0615650562

For Worldwide Distribution, Printed in the U.S.A

For Lynette - I love you. And for our three amazing kids...Alexa, Matthew, and Dani. And to my parents and GCC family for their continued love and support.

- C. Giacinto

For my darling wife, my future children and church leaders in training. May you learn to live in the fullness of grace.

- B. Conlan

CONTENTS

Foreword..i
Preface..v
Before You Begin..xi

1. How We Got Here..1
2. The Relationship Status..................................13
3. Have You Been MisTweeted?........................23
4. Power of the Key..41
5. The World's Largest Pulpit............................51
6. Friends and Followers....................................65
7. When it Matters...75
8. Rise of the Thumb Tribe................................93
9. God's Goal - Relationships..........................103
10. So...Now What?!?..113

Foreword

In *Cloud Culture,* Bryce and Chuck address one of the most relevant issues of our time; *Christians and Social Media.* Social Media is influencing the modern world in ways that our grandparents never would have imagined. The fact that a 28 year old Mark Zuckerberg is currently one of the richest people on the earth because he launched a somewhat ethereal new way for humanity to communicate is astounding.

The wake of Social Media has left many church leaders, parents and teachers scratching their heads wondering if they should be controlling and prohibiting, or encouraging and guiding this new frontier. Bryce and Chuck provide the answer, encouraging and guiding.

As an author, I am keenly aware of the power of the written word. Yet only being able to publish a book annually, I have realized the incredible power of daily building relationships with individuals around the world through social media. As I blog weekly, I constantly hear that people feel connected, as if they already know me, because social media has given an outlet where people can hear my heart on a day-by-day basis.

People are hungry for relationships, and especially for transparency from leaders. We do no favors by standing on a pedestal and acting perfect. It's only when we are brave enough to open our heart and communicate bravely that life is transferred to others.

It used to be that when I arrived at the airport and a pastor picked me up to speak at his church, he would ask me about my books. Now the first comments are, "I loved what you said last week on Facebook," "Your blog totally stretched me," "Sister so-and-so in my church has been printing out your insights online and passing them to me each Sunday." The world has changed and every Christian needs to consider the implications of these profound changes and how to be Christ's ambassadors in this new realm. Cloud Culture helps one to consider these changes.

This book is written concisely, with sharp insight, kingdom principles and clever wit. I read the manuscript in one sitting, which I appreciated because I had to get back to my Facebook. Seriously though, this book will make you laugh, make you think, and maybe even raise your personal standards for communication.

Jonathan Welton
Author of *Normal Christianity*

Preface

Many people imagine that when an author decides to write a book, they pack very lightly and head off to a remote mountain cabin for endless months, where the only sounds to disturb the placid air are that of nature and the click of an antiquated typewriter. After several months of isolation, the now victorious author emerges, walks into his publisher's office, and slams a fifty- pound manuscript on his publisher's desk. When the dust settles, the publisher opens to the first page as a warm glow radiates forth from the pages, as he reads words that will forever change the literary arts and take its proper place on a shelf between Homer and Shakespeare.

This, however, is not that book!

The book that you now hold in your hands is the result of a happy accident. While we fully believe that a conversation about the role of the Church in the age of social media is both worthwhile and necessary, we- the authors- had few intentions of initiating, nor facilitating that discussion.

To further this point, it's worth mentioning that we are not authors. Well, we are now, but by profession Chuck is the Worship Pastor of a church in Streator, IL, and Bryce is the owner of a digital media company in Chicago. The decision to write this book was the result of a snap decision that started mostly as a joke.

As the Story Goes

What you are about to read came, out of an honest conversation, that turned into an ongoing dialogue. And several months later, after innumerable emails and countless discussions via social media, those interactions became a book.

We have been acquaintances for several years, in that every fall we both participate in a large worship conference in Chicago. Chuck lends his talents on the guitar, and Bryce manages the conference media. At the 2011 conference, during a bit of down time in between sessions, Chuck was sharing with the group his growing concerns regarding believers and social media in that there has been a lack of dialogue in the Church on the subject; not only the practical application in our lives, how to share our faith through our communications, but also for Christians to see the vast and growing possibilities social media holds open to us as well. As the conversation escalated, Bryce posed a challenge saying, "You should write a book," to which Chuck replied, "I really should, but only if you'll help me".

Now usually in situations like this people go their separate ways and what seemed like a good idea at the moment never materializes. But this time it did. In fact, we have been diligent in turning our private conversations about a Christian's role in social media public, because we feel that this is a dialog that needs to be had. We feel strongly that everything the Bible teaches about words and communication can and **must** be applied to every current and emerging form of digital communication.

What to Expect

We've made an effort to avoid merely listing the dos and don'ts of social media. It is also worth stating that we have not written a manual for leveraging social media to maximize your success in terms of popularity or evangelism. So what is this book about? It's about taking the technologies and communication tools that make up a big part of your lives and examining how they fit into your lives as you live out His Kingdom on the earth, follow Him, and serve others. We've made an attempt to write in such a way that leaves room for the Holy Spirit to work in the reader's life and bring change if change is needed. In short, this book deals with the deeper motivations of the heart, asks a few hard questions, brings healing, and ultimately aims to revolutionize our digital lives. We're hopeful that the light bulb goes on above your head and that you begin to see the endless opportunities available to you through social media.

As we'll discuss later in the book, we chose the name *Cloud Culture* as a title because we feel that it embodies the subject well. The idea of cloud computing is growing - you know, universal connectedness to your files regardless of where you are. Well, we took that the same expression to describe the social media world - a place where we are all connected, all the time. When we started writing we didn't have a title in mind, but as we got deeper into the writing process *Cloud Culture* presented itself as the obvious choice. We also liked that just as the Israelites in the Old Testament followed the pillar of cloud in the wilderness -which was the presence of God- in that same way, we, as modern day believers have the privilege of following the presence of God into the cloud -meaning the digital world. But more on that later.

With the growing complexity of the Internet, we hope that *Cloud Culture* will serve as a guide to help you see where you fit into this digital puzzle, so that as the body of Christ, we can all walk the walk…and type the talk.

Before You Begin

From this book's inception, we have wrestled with who it is that we are specifically writing this for, and who stands to benefit from it the most. Who is the target audience for this book? Are these concepts geared towards teenagers? College students? Parents? Pastors or those involved in ministry? Well, the answer is…Yes! So, before we begin, we'd like to address each of you individually so you can understand up front how the concepts addressed in this book can best serve you as an individual. We wrote this book with you in mind…all of you.

Teenagers

CAN I HAVE YOUR ATTENTION PLEASE? I mean your FULL attention. Put down the cell phone, and no one gets hurt. You, my friends, are multi-tasking geniuses. You can somehow manage to continually update multiple forms of social media, while texting six friends at the same time, convince your parents that you heard what they just said to you, and still manage to break your all-time high score on Temple Run…all at once. (For those reading this book five years from now, Temple Run was an IPhone game app…for those of you reading this twenty-five years from now, an iPhone was a touch-screen cellular device you actually had to hold in your hand…primitive, I know…and for those reading this book fifty years from now, a book was…oh well).

OK, I'm just having a little fun with you. Look, you've proven you can juggle. We want to help you prioritize all of this in your lives so you can not only utilize it all, but also do so with integrity and in a way that honors God and allows you to reach your generation. At the same time we feel that having real and genuine relationships is every bit as important, no, more important than your digital presence online. Life is to be lived, not just posted. This book isn't long, and hopefully not too boring. (You've made it this far.) Take it in, absorb it, and let it shape you as well as create dialog with your friends…with your parents…with your youth group. YOU can help raise the bar and set a Godly standard for your generation. Do you believe that? ...We do! If you've made it through these two paragraphs without checking your phone, then we're good to go. Carry on!

College Students

Social media began with you in mind. Facebook, for example, was created by a college student and for college students. Social media, texting, instant messaging, have all become such an integrated part of your every day life that one recent study has found that graduating college students would be hesitant to accept a job from a company that would restrict social media access and 40% of you say you would take a lower salary to maintain your current social media freedoms[1]. This makes it difficult to determine whether social media is a hobby, a habit, or an addiction amongst your age group. Whichever it is, I think we can agree it is a huge priority in your life, and a big part of your every day. It is our hope that as college students and as a believers in Christ that you would take the concepts in this

---

[1] David Strom / November 2, 2011 http://www.readwriteweb.com/enterprise/2011/11/gen-y-demands-greater-work-fle.php

book very seriously. Social media and technology are not mere luxuries or entertainment for you. They are part of you now. You already "do" social media all day, every day. We want to help you do it better. Look, if you're already going to do it, you might as well change the world, right?

Parents

You have a unique and difficult two-fold role, in that you need to navigate your place in the world of technology and social media (which by the way, you may not have grown up with), while at the same time carrying the responsibility of parenting your kids through it as well. It means staying abreast of it all, above and beyond your personal use of it. It is our hope that this book can act as a bridge for dialog between you and your kids. While you function in your role as parent regarding your kid's access to technology, there is also much that you can learn from them in the area of social media since it is such a large part of their world and a language they already speak fluently. *Cloud Culture* doesn't act as the end-all authority on the subject of social media, but rather, to have a sound,

Biblically based discussion that can serve your family and create open dialog in your home.

Pastors

It is our hope that this book can serve you, and serve you well. We believe that this is a discussion that needs to be had in the Church sooner rather than later. Social media is a daily part of the lives of probably the majority of your congregation or those you minister to and with. The increasing number of ways that we can choose to communicate with others creates opportunities for many pitfalls in the realm of social media, and these new forms of communications are areas where people desperately need pastoring. We feel it's necessary that those in ministry realize not only what a great tool social media can be, but that we are in a position of opportunity and responsibility to teach the Body of Christ how to communicate well with these new platforms. After all, love is often conveyed through words and actions.

Though it may change forms along the way, the use of technology as a means for constant communication is not a trend. Not only is it here to stay, but it stands to increase with coming years. So, we hope the information that follows will get your wheels spinning, so to speak, and equip you with novel ideas to pastor this new frontier that has become so much a part of all of our lives. We understand that your time is valuable. So, if our compiling this concise book can help to act as a resource for you on the subject or help to arm you to be able to address this timely issue with confidence, well then we've hit our mark. Together, let's work to put God's people at a rightful place at the forefront of what is possible with social media. At the same time we can set a collective standard regarding communication that honors God in every way.

How We Got Here

Humor me and pretend that we're going to teach you something.

If we cut to the heart of it, this is not a book on social media. It's a book about communication -how to do it better, and how we as Christians can engage the world through the dynamic and ever-evolving world of social media. In the old days communication was fairly straightforward- my mouth moved, your ear listened, brain interpreted, and you responded. Back and forth we go. Yes, written text was always sort of "around" but we would argue that speech has been the primary form of communication for thousands of years.

A quick flip through the history books and it becomes apparent that until modern times the greater population never learned to read and write, and those who did usually held a high place in society. Daily journaling and writing for pleasure was far from common place since, for the vast majority of human history, writing was an expensive hobby as the inks, dyes, and paper sources were hard to come by.

That being said, virtually every ancient people kept a written record of their culture or, at the very least, a chronology of their kings. Most of these accounts were pictorial in nature and told a story through images that represented an idea rather than a phonetic alphabet. Over time the pictures were refined and standardized into a modern alphabet. Today, the Hebrew alphabet, for example, bares a striking resemblance to the pictorial characters of ancient Israel.

All things considered, widespread literacy is a relatively recent addition in the scope of human history. With the advent of the printing press in circa 1440[2], written text has become more accessible, and now more than ever we have incorporated it into every facet of our lives.

---

[2] http://en.wikipedia.org/wiki/Printing_press

Enter the Internet

It's probably the understatement of the century to say that the Internet has changed the way we do... everything. With the birth of cyber technology there has been a massive, global shift from the verbal societies of our collective past to a text-based future. With email, text messaging, Facebook, Twitter, LinkedIn, blogs, and the thousands of other Internet destinations (not to mention their Christian counterparts) our fingers are constantly dancing across a keyboard. Remember the days when your cell phone had numbers on it and you couldn't check your email on your phone? Weird right? Everyone has been touched by this technology to some degree. Right now, I'm sitting in a coffee shop tapping this chapter out on my iPad's virtual keyboard... a virtual keyboard- seriously?

So what's the point? Well, it's basically this: we're living in a digital age, and many people have failed to transfer etiquette and socially acceptable practices into their digital lives. But if you're looking for a book that discourages the use of social media by Christians, I'm sorry to tell you that you won't find it here. Actually, we believe that as Christians we should be on the forefront of social media. After all, it's easy to argue that the only thing worth sharing is the Gospel (more on that in chapter 5 – "The World's Largest Pulpit"). You will also hear us reiterate over and over again the importance of face-to-face communication, and when to choose the old-fashioned route over the new high tech one.

All in all, social media in the digital age has made it possible to reach virtually every person on the planet with a demonstration of the Gospel and the unified message of hope and love. Which begs the question – What's the message that we're tweeting?

You Have Been Given a Voice

Considering the many benefits social media provides us all, such as the ability to connect with others, engage in entertainment, and promote and market ourselves or our goods, I am convinced that the greatest benefit provided is the one that speaks most deeply to something inside of us all. The greatest gift that social media has given to individuals is a "voice". People want to have a voice: to be heard and seen for that matter. They want to know that what they have to say is worth something and matters to someone. And ultimately, deep down, we all want to do or be a part of something significant. Social media has provided every individual a voice in a way that has never been available before. Singers no longer need a record label or radio airplay to be heard all over the world. Artists and photographers no longer need elusive gallery space to be seen. And anyone with an opinion can now have a platform and an audience without boundaries. In

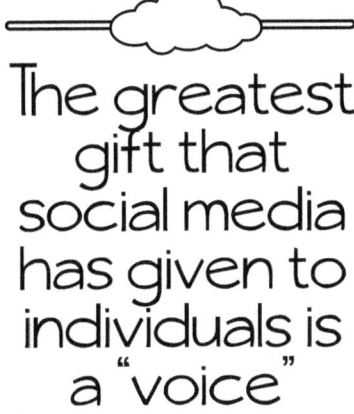

The greatest gift that social media has given to individuals is a "voice"

1 Corinthians, Paul mentions the compulsion he felt to preach the Gospel.

"Yet when I preach the gospel, I cannot boast, for I am compelled to preach. Woe to me if I do not preach the gospel!

- 1 Cor. 9:16 (NIV)

Social media will be used in one way or another because of the limitless possibility it provides. And you, as a believer, have been given an incredible gift through social media that is impossible to ignore. You have been given a voice. How are you using it?

No one can tell you how to use social media since it's your personal platform to the world. You get to express yourself as an individual. But what if the goal is bigger than merely having people see your online presence and realize that you love Jesus? But instead, can you imagine what would happen if you and I became a living, breathing, peer-to-peer network for the Gospel. It would mean the realization that you have the chance to speak directly into the lives of countless family, friends, friends of friends, and total strangers. That opportunity, my friends, is a gift. You have a voice…use it to be the love of Christ through your smart phone and your keyboard!

Teenagers, college students…can I speak directly to you for a moment? Our culture and society treat this stage in your life as mostly transitional – meaning, you are expected to be thinking seriously about your future. Who will you become someday…when you're all grown up? Expectations are rather low for this stage in your life, and that's unfortunate. As a Church, we aim to teach and train you so that one day in the future you will be strong and faith-filled adults, as if your lives right now are only in preparation for what is to come. You are not just a group of potentials, but rather, you have within you - right now - the ability to dynamically shape the world around you. God entrusted some of the biggest, world changing responsibilities to people your age in the Bible. By studying the Rabbinic culture of Jesus' time, and applying it to the Gospel account, I'm convinced that most of Jesus original twelve disciples were not a bunch of old guys with beards, as traditional art would suggest. Instead, I would suggest to you that they were most likely around your age when they started following Jesus. Most scholars agree that Mary would have been in her teens when she carried Jesus. David was probably a teenager when he slew Goliath [1 Samuel 17:155] and Jeremiah the prophet was rebuked by God for thinking that because he was young he couldn't be used powerfully [Jeremiah 1:6]. I could go on and on. So don't think for one minute God can't use you in a huge way right now or that your voice doesn't matter. In 1 Timothy 4:12, God instructs his disciple Timothy to…

"Let no one despise your youth, but be an example to the believers in word, in conduct, in love, in spirit, in faith, in purity…"

-1 Timothy 4:12 (NKJV)

Your faith is much more than a box you check that denotes that you are a Christian as opposed to subscribing to Buddhism, the Islamic faith, or a host of others. Instead, your faith in Christ is supposed to be the very core of your being and not merely what you represent, where your convictions lie, or a philosophy you agree with. This is who you are. And because of the supremacy of Christ in your life, it is important that you realize that your words, comments, links, and posts go out and become part of other's daily lives. What an incredible gift and responsibility you have been given - a gift that shouldn't be squandered or labeled as ordinary.

Adults, parents - it's your turn. You may not have grown up with these technologies, but your kids, well, they don't know any other way. You've watched the rate of communication technology advance to the point that now it's difficult to keep up. So try as you might to tame the digital beast you've probably discovered along the way that the digital world isn't going to wait for you to catch up… and neither will your kids. You walk the line of learning, using, and parenting simultaneously, while feeling three steps behind your kids at every turn. The integration of the digital and the physical will only increase with successive generations, and it's ok if you don't feel that you can keep up with the pace at which technology and communication advance. Regardless of how connected or disconnected you may feel, you can still set into place practices that show examples of integrity and Kingdom living in the technologies that you are involved with. It's quality over quantity. The measure of how well you do the social platforms that you're on is far more significant than being on every new social media site that pops up. You are still able to have a serious impact on others while at the same time demonstrating proper and effective use of social media to your kids. Now, before you plan your dinner-table tirade and institute mandatory family social media classes, let me say in fair warning, that in my experience with social media, adults are often been the worst offenders of inappropriate social media use. Among a variety of contributing factors is the fact that social media is an abbreviated form of written communication which merits a slew of etiquette and protocols, many of them unvoiced, which adults are expected to somehow learn as they go along. And more often than not, we end up learning the hard way. Suddenly, what seemed like a nifty new way to catch up with the latest happenings becomes a pathway heavy laden with potential pitfalls. Miscommunications, unintentional offenses, and complete misunderstandings, are but a few of the many ways adults fail completely in using social media. I feel for you; it's like we're asking you to play jazz with Louis Armstrong when you've only learned a few of the most basic music scales.

Keep in mind that you have a voice as well, and I encourage you to use it with great discernment not only with the intention of being an example to your kids (that's just a positive byproduct) but also with the realization that there is more to using social media as a child of God than just having a public bulletin board of our daily events, interests, self or business promotions. All of those things are wonderful and necessary, but as our faith in Christ grows to be the center of our being, we should expect to see that part of our lives spill over into our presence in social media.

The Relationship Status

Ah yes, the relationship status in social media: married, single, complicated, or none whatsoever. This is where the rubber meets the road, because it's not official until it's Facebook-official. If you're the exceedingly clever type, you might assume that we're trying to convince you to inject your beliefs into your online presence because, well, you should. But in the end, if all you walk away with is a feeling of obligation to start posting a daily scripture online, strictly out of a sense of duty as a result of reading this book, then we have not only failed, but we've failed miserably. The end result should not be that all of your friends, family and other connections exclaim in uniform exasperation,

"OK, we get it, you're a Christian!"

Spillover

When someone is in a relationship, it naturally spills over into social media. Their status changes, their posts change, their daily events change, and they inevitably update their profile pic to include their newly found romantic interest. Everything about their lives in social media reflects the fact that they are in a relationship. The relationship can't help but present itself in a natural, non-obligatory way. The relationship itself and the place it holds in the lives of the smitten is one of significance that is displayed with pride. Whenever people attempt to hide or neglect to mention key relationships in their social media presence, there is almost assuredly something wrong with the relationship. Ultimately, social media is the place for our relationships: the close and the casual, the intimate and the distant. It's a place to gather the people you know, as well as develop relationships and interact with folks you've never actually met. The casual ones can be found buried deep in our profiles, but the truly close relationships in our lives are an ever-present reality that we are proud to display on a daily basis. And in the end isn't that what using social media is really all about?

Our intent is not to give you tips and ideas on how to better fuse your Christian vocabulary into social media. Rather, we'd like to remind you that you are in the most important relationship of all! A relationship with the living God. *That* is your ultimate relationship status- and it shouldn't feel like work, require any tips, or out of the box thinking for that to be known. Your presence in social media may certainly include every detail about your daily life that you want it to (from the notable to the mundane). But since you are in a relationship with God, your presence in social media should be the same as your presence on the Earth - a direct outpouring of a life of worship, faith, and love of the One who gives you life. If we can manage to carry on daily in social media, and those we interact with remain unaware of our affections for the Almighty, then we're just taking up space...virtually as well as physically.

Status: Complicated

As we've established, being a Christian isn't merely a box on all your social profiles. You are not part of a demographic; you are in relationship with the living God. Ask yourself this question- "Does my life in social media show that I'm in THIS relationship?" There are many people who identify with Christianity as a worldview but that's not what we're talking about here. Does your presence in social media show HIS presence in your life?

How would you feel if you got married and your spouse's Facebook page neglected to show any trace of you or your relationship? I suppose I can only speak for myself when I say that the amount of devastation that would bring me is unimaginable. It would be a strong indication of some deep issues, wouldn't it? If you are engaged to be married, I would think that your excitement, planning, and love for your fiancé would be hard to miss. If you're in high school, you might feel the same way about your senior prom: posting updates, taking pictures of your dress, and chatting with your friends

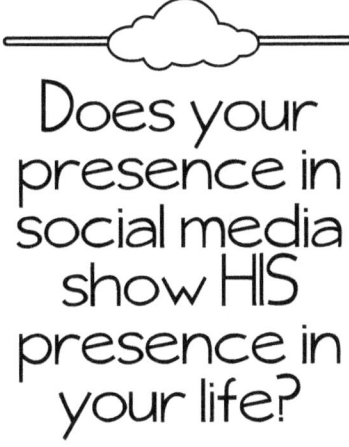

Does your presence in social media show HIS presence in your life?

about how great it's going to be. The point is that any truly significant relationship in your life that you manage to keep off of social media almost requires a concerted effort. The Bible says that you are the Bride of Christ and He is your Bridegroom[3]. How can this relationship status not only permeate, but also govern your communications and use of technology as well? This isn't evangelism training for the online world. Social media is about relationships, and this is the relationship of all relationships.

---

[3] Eph 5:25-27, 2Cor 11:22, Rev. 19:7-9, Rev. 21:9,

As we've stressed already, this is not an invitation to find more ways to incorporate your faith into social media. Instead, go deeper in your relationship with Him, and you will find that you will have a further reaching, deeper impact in the lives of others via social media. It's through the depth of your relationship with Him and making Him famous that draws people to Christ in an authentic way. In turn, you will become a better representative of Christianity than you ever would by trying to cleverly squeeze God into every post.

People are generally pretty good at spotting the genuine article and there is a noticeable difference between social media as a natural extension of an intimate relationship with God and someone who is just pushing a Jesus-centered agenda. We should strive against merely using social media as only a platform for voicing our beliefs and opinions. When we only do that, it just gets lost in all the noise. After all, we're not looking to replace one meaningless message with another. Rather, we have *the* message and it would be good to get that message out.

…and the world is watching

When U.S. ambassadors takes up residency in another country, they become a representative of their country at all times during the course of their stay. Their title is not reserved only for official meetings or speeches, but is valid in every conversation, at every meal, and in every moment of their daily life. To further the point, ambassadors' job descriptions are to be constant representations of the country from which they have been sent. Until the moment they leave their country of residence, their title remains: Ambassador of the United States of America.

In a letter to the Corinthians, the apostle Paul writes,

"Now then, we are ambassadors for Christ, as though God were pleading through us: we implore you on Christ's behalf, be reconciled to God"

- 2 Corinthians 5:20 (NKJV)

He also tells us,

"For our citizenship is in heaven, from which we also eagerly wait for the Savior, the Lord Jesus Christ,"
- Philippians 3:20 (NKJV)

It's clear from the Scriptures provided that one of the many things that happened as a result of the Cross is that you and I have become ambassadors of Jesus and the Kingdom of God. From the moment you were saved, just like a real-life ambassador, you became a representative of Jesus at all times - whether you are consciously deciding to be or not. The world is always watching. Sure there are times of active witnessing, when we speak of our faith in social media or give words that encourage another. But we are also an open witness when we tear someone down or post questionable material as well. Even worse is when people (Christians) use status updates and tweets as a platform for passive-aggressive disagreement.

Maybe you've watched from the sidelines as two people carry on a public disagreement online, or maybe you've found yourself in the middle of a few along the way. It can be remarkably easy to get sucked into such altercations. And while certain behaviors may seem socially acceptable under the guise of the 'right of self-expression,' not only are we bound to the ramifications of our words, but such conversations need to be held up against the light of Scripture. Picture if you will, two believers having a spat via social media over something personal, scriptural, political, relational, or regarding the Church. If one of those involved in the dispute has 400 friends in their network and the other has 500 friends in theirs, then you can expect that 900 bystanders have potentially been exposed to the Body of Christ at work in a horrible way. Even if the two involved settle their disagreement quickly, the fallout from their embroilment may leave a negative and long-lasting impression on those who were witness to it all. The sad reality is that in just a few moments, and a couple careless keystrokes later, irreparable damage has been done to people's feelings and reputations.

I promise that the world **is** watching. And while they may not understand Christian-eze, they do understand discord. They understand dysfunction, division, and animosity as well. At times it may require a tremendous level of restraint to prevent yourself from lashing out publicly, but I encourage you to let the Holy Spirit dictate when and how to handle any issue that may come up rather than relying on your emotions.

To me, the rise of social media has proven one thing: that mankind has tried to streamline and create new opportunities for something that has always been and always will be. As we'll explore in later chapters, we are hardwired for relationships. And social media is designed to help us facilitate those relationships. The chief relationship, however - the one that determines how we relate to everyone around us- is the one that we each get to have with Jesus Christ. And that is the one that really counts.

Have You Been MisTweeted?

A few years back my family and I (Chuck) went on a missions trip to Nakuru, Kenya. One particular evening at Solid Rock Church, I was scheduled to give the evening message. Needless to say, I don't speak a lick of Swahili, and so aside from a few universal hand signals, I had no way of communicating with the people without the assistance of a translator. Fortunately, there was a translator present, and I was able to deliver my sermon in English.

Up to that point, my only experience working with a translator was during a trip to China, when my wife, Lynette, and I adopted our youngest daughter years prior. Our Chinese translator spoke on our behalf throughout the adoption process, and we were more like bystanders kept on hand to answer the occasional question than actual participants in the conversation. Let me assure you that it was a completely different experience from addressing a large crowd through the use of a translator. As it turns out, speaking through a translator is a difficult task if you're not accustomed to it. I had to make major adjustments to how I delivered the sermon, even though I had given it once before and felt quite comfortable with it. Speaking through a translator also put a surprising amount of stress on my brain since I had to alter my thinking process to make sure that every word, every statement, was reduced to it's simplest form while maintaining it's intended meaning. It's a literal downsizing of vocabulary, while trying to keep the context intact. The best way I can describe it is, if you were about to paint a picture and someone took most of the colors off the palette. I was crippled in terms of how I had usually communicated, since I couldn't ramble on to make a point like I could to an English speaking audience. On top of all that, there were the cultural barriers, and my references for illustration, which might make perfect sense to an American audience meant nothing in central Kenya. Sure, it may look easy if you've never had the opportunity to speak to a crowd of people who speak a different language than you. The speaker says a few words, and then the translator says the same thing in another language. The transaction is complete, and the speaker may continue when he sees the crowd nod and smile with complete understanding. Right? I wish! Communicating through a translator is a very stop-and-go format that is difficult to explain. You have to interrupt your thought process every few words, which makes it quite difficult to maintain a steady stream of thought. Further, context is much more difficult to achieve when there's no platform for elaboration, and I found myself often feeling frustrated by the process.

    As difficult as it was, I was entertained as I watched the translator take my best attempt to express a thought and reframe it to mean something to the Kenyan believers who sat before me. And who should I be directing my remarks to? I didn't know if I was supposed to look at the audience I was speaking to, or the poor soul who was trying to decipher the point I was trying to get across. I remember how on more than one occasion he paused, laughed a little, and looked up at the ceiling while he tried to figure out how he was going to translate what I had said into Swahili. It's a strange dynamic, but a wonderful way to communicate all at the same time. I suppose that the sermon, even with everything it had going against it, went about as well as it could have gone, and I learned a profound lesson that night about the importance of context when it comes to transmitting ideas from one person to another.

One of the byproducts of modern communication and social networking has been that our language and vocabulary have been compacted. Abbreviated words and shortened sentence structure, for the sake of time and convenience, have ultimately resulted in the loss of context. Considering that the English language is only comprised of twenty-six letters to begin with, along with the fact that most people struggle to communicate effectively when speaking face to face, it's no wonder that people are feeling a little lost in translation. We should not be surprised to discover that abbreviated texts, tweets, and Facebook posts, which not only lack detail but also strip words of their contextual surroundings, leave readers with the unreasonable responsibility of reading between the lines in order to gain understanding.

Scientific researchers who study verbal and non-verbal communication have proven that the high majority of our communication is, in fact, nonverbal. While studies differ slightly in their findings, we can safely say that approximately two-thirds of our total communication is conveyed non-verbally[4]. As interesting as that may be, the studies take on a whole new life when we consider that many of these studies were conducted before e-mails, texts, and social networks like Facebook and Twitter had been added to our lives as primary forms of communication. So, while it may seem like streamlining our language into a more concise format for digital mediums is a logical step in the evolution of communication, we have yet to develop an accurate way to communicate context. It is difficult to fault the recipient of a text or post for misinterpreting a statement when they really weren't given much to work with in the first place.

---

[4] "Nonverbal Communication" By Albert Mehrabian/Publisher: Walter De Gruyter Inc/Copyright June 1972

"A word aptly spoken is like apples of gold in settings of silver"

- Prov. 25:11 (NIV)

Merriam-Webster's Collegiate® Dictionary defines *aptly* as "suited to a purpose…" With this in mind, let's re-read the proverb.

"A word 'suited to a purpose' is like apples of gold in settings of silver."

This is difficult to accomplish when we text, post, vent, and express ourselves in an abbreviated and often vague format.

We are privileged to live in the most technologically advanced age in human history, with tools of communication that no previous generation could have dreamed of. As believers, we would be wise to take seriously the power of our words, and give thought to every utterance. When we get lazy for the sake of time or convenience and abbreviate our speech in excess, we inadvertently leave room for misunderstandings. Further, when we condense our written thoughts out of emotion, we risk seriously damaging our relationships with others. Proverbs tells us that

"The heart of the righteous weighs its answers..."
- Proverbs 15:28a (NIV)

    Did you catch that? To weigh our words is to give careful thought to what we say before we say it. It means to take other people's feelings into account and consider the ramifications our words may have. Face to face communication is difficult enough to convey properly our thoughts and intents. Texts and online postings add an entirely different dimension to interpersonal communication that often isn't an appropriate platform for serious thought. There are many Scriptures like the one above that pertain to the power of our words and our communication, which only serve to demonstrate the importance. From this generation on, **this** is how we will communicate with each other and with the world around us. We believe that there should be a standard for digital communication in the Body of Christ, and that this generation is the one that will lay the groundwork for generations to come. Collectively, we have a decision to make. Will we create a culture of integrity and honor that builds lasting relationships within the digital realms, or will social media continue to exist as a segregated part of each of our lives reserved for gossip, empty chatter, and entertainment?

    I've lost count of how many times I've watched as people text each other from across the room. With unlimited texting plans available on the cheap, it's become easier than walking over to them and having a conversation. I often joke, "You know, that message had to travel to space and back?" It is well known among the cellular service industry that the average American teen sends over 3,000 texts per month[5] with those numbers rising. The adult population is not far behind, with texting

---

[5] Study: Many Teens Sending 3,000 Texts A Month / April 21, 2010/Ben Tracy/ http://www.cbsnews.com/2100-18563_162-6415699.html

among adults rising 75% in the past year alone. As staggering as the numbers are, this is only a study on texting, and doesn't factor in Twitter, FaceBook, e-mail, and every other digital exchange done on a daily basis. We are literally inundated with our various forms of communication, most of which are based on convenience rather than solidifying and developing real relationships. Further, given the startling rate of social media growth over the last ten years leads every forward thinking individual to the eventual conclusion that social media is here to stay. And it's only just begun.

This is why we need to have this dialog now. It is high time that we as Christians give careful consideration to the power that is at our fingertips and the manner in which we present ourselves, conduct ourselves, and represent the Kingdom of God. It is time to redeem communication.

Digital Etiquette

While there are various forms of etiquette slowly growing within online social networks, we believe the

Body of Christ can, and presumably should be, on the forefront of setting high standards for the appropriate use of social media in terms of how and when we use it. This is one area where the Body of Christ simply cannot afford to be the last on board. Believers should know and understand better than anyone the power of our words and conversations. When we text, e-mail, or post out of emotion without weighing our answers as the Bible instructs, we leave too much room to hurt others as well as do damage to our own reputations. Have you noticed it's rather difficult to take back a text after you've hit the send key? Gossip and chatter are dreadfully damaging when spoken, let alone when permanently etched into the digital walls of profiles and updates. Stories change, details get exaggerated, and people get hurt. With texting and social networks encouraging you to speak your mind in 140

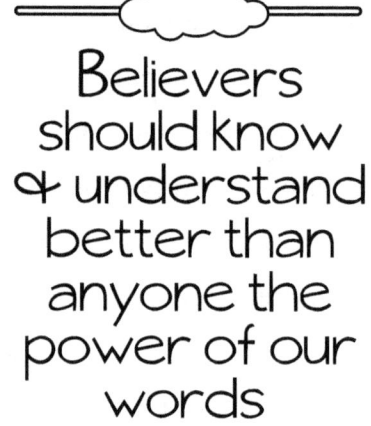

Believers should know & understand better than anyone the power of our words

characters or less, details chip away and context gets lost. Often times, this leads to people making judgments and assumptions about the one who posted the comment. In the past, stories were passed one at a time from person to person with interactions and questions that helped the hearer discover the teller's true intent. Today, one slightly vague tweet or Facebook post can hit hundreds if not thousands of family, friends, and acquaintances in a matter of seconds, which puts everyone who sees it in the position to individually wrestle with, interpret, and ultimately judge what they've just read.

Context is especially difficult when letters are all we have to work with. RIGHT NOW I AM SHOUTING! You may know this due to my use of capital letters, since using capital letters excessively is culturally understood now as raising one's voice. But besides the caps lock key, there is little else that clearly communicates the heart or intent of the person beyond the actual words they type. Of course, someone could use all caps because it's easier for them to read, without ever realizing what caps might convey to their reader.

By analogy, we are still in the "Wild West" stages of digital communication. And there is a certain amount of shooting from the hip going on. Simply because it's **social** media, there probably always will be. But this haphazard behavior becomes more apparent when people can hide behind aliases and usernames. But make no mistake; even though we sometimes comment under the anonymity of a username, we are responsible for our communication. Our opinion, remark, comment, or agreement with something or someone online is a powerful thing, living on long after we even remember the comment itself.

So what's the answer then? Is it necessary to completely explain ourselves every time we want to "like" someone's status update, profile picture or new viral video of a kitten doing something cute? Honestly, I guess that depends on the circumstances and who might be involved. Sometimes the difference between being understood and misunderstood, or worse, being taken completely out of context, could be as little as five words - or a forgotten comma. In these cases, it's worth taking few extra seconds to read over that text or post before pulling the trigger.

That second glance could be all you need to cause you to rethink your post and edit it appropriately.

In Related News...

Our culture has become addicted to the sound-byte. The world of news, politics, and entertainment, are based on carefully chosen bits of quotes and information, where context is not nearly as important as latching onto key phrases and hot button topics to drive ratings. For example, a politician may speak for a full thirty minutes in a press conference about important issues concerning the wellness and future of an entire local community but what makes the news or goes viral on YouTube is the five-second gaffe that unintentionally offends a whole group of people. Just as a public figure's life and reputation can be damaged by one sentence lifted from *The New York Times* without consideration for context, we are all now, in a sense, in that same fragile position. This is a time in history when people can be famous just for being famous and there are dozens of celebs-of-the-moment that have become famous by effectively using the voices granted to them through social media. While most of us will never become famous, social media has created a place for everyone to be seen and to be heard without regard to who you are, how much money you have, or how popular you are. Everyone has an opportunity to be heard. You get your very own soapbox and an audience that will listen and also interact with you. Your presence in social media could easily be compared to your own personal reality show where you are the director, producer, and the star. You get to decide what sort of content gets released through your channel, what you will share, and what you won't. I have a sneaking suspicion, however, that some of the best, most integrity filled posts are often the ones that are never posted. The great champion of Protestantism, Martin Luther said it best-

"You are not only responsible for what you say, but also for what you do not say"[6]

-Martin Luther

They are the comments that you choose not to make; the ones when you can step back, take a deep breath, and decide that it's just not worth the hurt it might cause. It's a true sign of maturity and Christian character when you can restrain yourself from leaving remarks that will only fuel the online conversations which are neither edifying nor productive. The moments when you choose not to participate in inter-web entanglements, as difficult as that may be, are the times when we show the greatest level of strength and look the most like Jesus. This is especially difficult if you feel as though you have been the target of someone else's post. But take heart; Jesus himself was the target of much scorn, and the Holy Spirit can give you the strength to endure it gracefully.

---

[6] http://www.brainyquote.com/quotes/quotes/m/martinluth383752.html © 2001 - 2012 BrainyQuote / BookRags Media Network

Sometimes, picking up the phone or speaking even briefly face to face, provides all of the context necessary to clear up a miscommunication. We are encouraged in Hebrews 12:14,

14 Make every effort to live in peace with everyone and to be holy; without holiness no one will see the Lord. (NIV)

Sometimes this means that you have to be the bigger person, and make an effort to settle the conflict in an honorable way - even if you think that you are in the right or feel vicimized by the other person's actions. Healthy discussion is a great thing. Even debate can be productive and there are certainly subjects worth defending. On the other hand, pick your battles, and let little things be exactly that… little things. If you feel stuck, pray for wisdom and let God fulfill His promise to us.

"If any of you lacks wisdom, let him ask of God, who gives to all liberally and without reproach, and it will be given to him"

- James 1:5 (NKJV)

Do what you can to let your online presence be clear and easily understood, and avoid posts that could be a potential stumbling block for someone else.

When I think about communicating through modern technology and social media, I think of that night in Africa. I think about the fact that in order to communicate effectively through social media, there needs to be an internal translation process that breaks down our complex thoughts into their simplest form. It would benefit us, not to mention the world around us, if we integrate that very unnatural, stop-and-go process to every post, comment, and update. There is a great value in slowing down and thinking through every word carefully. Lastly, consider that while a statement might make perfect sense in your own mind, it may not come across the same at all in a text, a post, or in Swahili for that matter.

Power of the Key

Death and life are in the power of the... keystroke? I know...that's not what the Bible says. What it does say in Proverbs is,

"Death and life are in the power of the tongue, and those who love it will eat its fruit."

- Proverbs 18:21(NKJV)

So the question is, can we take Scripture, along with it's wisdom, principles, and spiritual significance, and apply it to technologies and social media that were previously non-existent? Is the Bible itself not written Word? When the deaf speak using sign language, are their words not just as real and meaningful as those spoken audibly? Understand, spoken language does not originate in the mouth anyway, nor does the tongue speak on it's own. In his Gospel, Matthew states;

"But the things that proceed out of the mouth come from the heart."

- Matt 15:18a (NASB)

The heart, which in Western mind-sets, is the emotional center, tells the brain what to feel, and the brain translates those feelings into concepts and words. The tongue does not act alone with regards to speech, but it does manifest with words the complexities of the hidden, inner life inside each one of us. While the word "tongue" in Proverbs 18:21 refers to the muscle in your mouth, it's clear that it represents our tool of verbal speech. In scripture the word "tongue" is also translated ten times to mean "language". In other words, if our tongue is a tool, as is language, then it stands to reason that keystrokes must certainly be included as well. Other verses in Proverbs 18 refer to man's words, his mouth, his lips, pleading cases, and tale bearing. In other words…Communication!

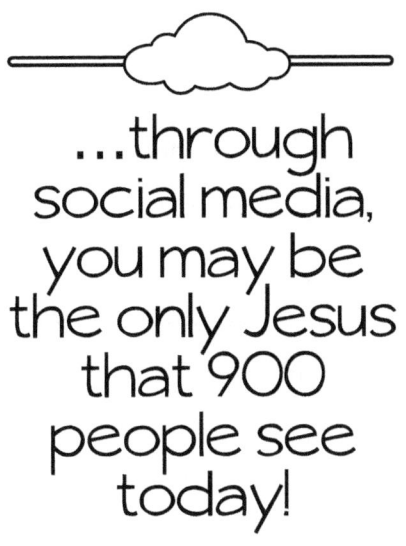

...through social media, you may be the only Jesus that 900 people see today!

Whether we speak with our mouth, sign with our hands, write with a pen, text or type, it not only stands to reason that we are responsible for our communications, but also the power our words hold (a power regardless of whether that method of communication is old or new). As technology moves further into a voice recognition based platform, the tongue once again becomes a primary format of delivery anyway. My point is that regardless of the format or applied technology for communicating, our words hold tangible power. When I read Proverbs 18, I don't merely see a piece of good advice. Instead, what I see is that my communications, in whatever form they may appear, are real and alive in both the physical and the spiritual realms.

I'm a big fan of the face-to-face conversation when it comes to important matters. That doesn't mean I overly enjoy confrontation. I don't. For some people, it's like a sport. But I do recognize that it is sometimes necessary, tends to encourage integrity, and is the best choice regarding important matters over texts or social media threads. (See the chapter titled "When It Matters".) Now, don't misunderstand me. This certainly doesn't mean that there isn't a proper context in social media for important matters, opinions, and expression. Of course there is, and we should express ourselves as Believers with great confidence and clarity. But we should not take lightly the power of our words, even with the most leisurely-added post on Facebook. Your contribution to Internet-land has the power to affect people's moods, their day, their views, their opinion of you or someone else, and maybe even shake or encourage someone's faith for that day.

Have you ever heard the phrase "you may be the only Jesus that a person sees today?" As this still applies to every interpersonal interaction, it's important to recognize that through social media, you may be the only Jesus that

900 people see today! Did you get that? Are we speaking life and blessing into the hearts of others? Or worse, are we tearing people down, or just making a bunch of noise and not actually saying anything?

As I'm writing this, I've been monitoring (and participating in) some Facebook activity that is one of the best illustrations I've ever seen for what's possible in the hands and hearts of those who understand the power at their fingertips. Someone I know, who I consider a man of faith, has been battling cancer for a long time. Over the past few years he has constantly posted detailed messages of faith and the goodness of God through his trials. It's been a privilege to be continuously uplifted and encouraged by someone going through so much. At the time of this writing, my friend is in his final hours. Collectively, people from all around the world are pouring personal messages of prayer, encouragement, faith, and stories into him via his Facebook wall, and they are being read aloud to him as he drifts in and out. What a tremendous picture of the Body of Christ from a distance acting in a way that only modern technology could allow. For all of the mistakes I see people make online - the lack of etiquette, decency, discretion, and often common sense - it is great to see that there are many in the Body of Christ who get it. They have realized the power their words hold, and the privilege they have been given to speak life and blessing into the lives of others.

Allow me to illustrate. I can take a hammer in my hand, and either build a house or tear one down. Either way, the hammer itself is amoral - neither good nor evil. It's a neutral tool. What the tool becomes when it's in my hand, however, is an extension of the intensions of my heart. It's the same with our words in the realm of social media. Do your words pour out as constant negativity, or do they restore life with every written line? Are your words generally empty? Or, do they build up and encourage those who read them? Here's what I'd like you to do. Put this book down for about fifteen minutes. I know it'll take great strength to pry yourself away from our astonishing brilliance, but for the next fifteen minutes go back over your own online presence for the past couple of weeks (via Facebook, Twitter, blogs, comments, posts, etc.) and read them as though you're a stranger coming across a random profile. Do your best to ignore what you already know about each post and read the words that you've actually written. What do they say about you? In only about fifteen minutes, you should be able to learn a lot about this person (you). Seriously - go ahead! This book isn't going anywhere.

15 minute break...

I'm going to assume you followed through on this challenge. What did you learn about yourself? In a lot of ways, your presence online is a mirror of who you are, what you're like, and what's important to you. Is your faith as present as you'd like it to be? Are you generally edifying and positive? Does your online presence reveal that you have the answer for a lost and dying world?

We have tremendous tools in our hands that no previous generation in their wildest dreams could have imagined. It's time we realize the power that is at our disposal and the difference that one small voice can make. You can be a conduit of life, blessing, encouragement, and a force for the Kingdom of God. On the other hand, you can be just another person in a sea of empty and pointless posts, opinions, and updates that no one is really interested in anyway.

Consider, when Jesus walked up to some fisherman and said, "Follow Me, and I will make you fishers of men." He could have said that He would make them a lot of things, but He said "fishers." He took the very thing they already were doing, the thing they were good at, the way they spent their days, the thing they enjoyed, and redefined it for His purpose and blew it up! As you know already, they dropped their nets and followed to become fishers of a different kind. Certainly they had the choice to stay behind, and probably would have had a decent and ordinary life. But by choosing to become His kind of fisher, those ordinary men changed the world. Jesus literally took the disciples' every day activity, a mundane and routine practice, and transformed it for His purpose. They went from fishing…to FISHING!

Let's say, for example, that social media is like a giant swimming pool that is very crowded at the 'shallow' end. By 'shallow' I'm referring to the high percentage of self-serving posts, comments, expressed opinions, and pictures that make up a high majority of what's posted each day. Another way of looking at it is to see it as content that brings more attention to the one posting than to contribute anything useful or beneficial to those who see it.

Consider the fact that most of us intermittently spend an enormous part of our day in this metaphoric pool. While many are content to splash around in the shallow end, as Christians, we have an opportunity to follow Him into the deep end. We can either allow communications, in whatever form they are, to remain routine and mundane, or we can drop our nets, and let Him revolutionize and transform our communications for His purpose. Make the choice today not to make the shallow end of the pool the place you live, but rather, where you cast your net.

Do you believe that? Do you believe that there could be a higher purpose for the tools at our disposal than simply playing games and letting people know where we had lunch? I want to create an image in your mind. The next time you are about to post an update in a social media form (Twitter, Facebook, etc.) I want you to imagine you have all of your Facebook friends, Twitter followers, and so on, together in one room. You have their attention for a few seconds out of every day. You have this captive audience of hundreds (maybe thousands for some of you). At which point you stand up in front of this crowd and declare, "I have something to say to you all. Now that I have your attention, what I'd like you to know today is…I'm shopping right now." Ok, I know, there's nothing wrong with shopping, and there's certainly nothing wrong with tweeting about it, or any of your other daily moments that aren't exactly newsworthy. But I did want to give you a visual of the captive and expansive audience you have at your disposal every time you sign in. And, amidst our routine, lighter moments in life…amidst our fishing…don't miss the opportunity to truly cast your net and go FISHING.

The World's Largest Pulpit

In July of 2009, the US Census Bureau announced that the population of the United States had grown to 307,006,550 people - and Jesus commanded His disciples to make disciples of all of them. Wow! Can you imagine how different the world would be if all 300 million people in the United States believed? It would send monumental shockwaves throughout the nations, transforming societies, eradicating social injustices (human trafficking and starvation), ending wars, and establishing on the earth the Kingdom of God, which is clearly seen through love, abundance, and generosity.

Like most people, I long to see the fulfillment of the promise that God made through the prophet Habakkuk when he said,

*"For the earth will be filled
With the knowledge of the glory of the Lord,
As the waters cover the sea."*

- Habakkuk 2:14 (NKJV)

To illustrate, I'll borrow the imagery of the ocean floor. There's not a lot of dry real estate on the bottom of the ocean - and this is how the earth will be filled with the knowledge of the Glory of the Lord. Gives new meaning to the word "saturate" doesn't it?

"But how is this even possible?" I wonder to the Lord. The sheer amount of time and resources and manpower it would take to reach the whole earth for the Lord is staggering in scope. "If only there were a place to reach them all at once....". As you've probably guessed - there is. At the time of this writing, Facebook alone has over 850 million daily active users. That's two and a half times the total population of the United States actively using Facebook to interact with the world. Of the 850 million[7], approximately 600 million (75%) of them reside outside the United States. Twitter, the micro-blogging platform, gains 600,000[8] new users every day on average! While the numbers clearly show the incredible global addiction to social media, for Christians, it does something else. It literally brings the nations of the world into our home and office, and puts everyone with an Internet connection within reach. Never before in the history of mankind have we had such an opportunity to speak into the lives of virtually every person on the planet. With Facebook being the undisputed king of social media at the time of this book's writing, with Twitter not far behind, and new social media sites springing up every day, our lives as Christians have taken an interesting turn into the realms of technology.

When talking about social media, it's important to remember that it is socially oriented, unlike the program-oriented world we're a part of. What this means, is that

---

[7] http://newsroom.fb.com/content/default.aspx?NewsAreaId=22 © 2012 Facebook

[8] "Who's Winning The Tweet Game" © Zeta 2010 http://www.zeta.net/social-marketing/the-tweet-game.html

when people want to get the latest breaking news, they'll turn to a news network. Or, if they need the weather, they'll check with Weather.com. Program-oriented services provide a specific type of information at any given time. Programs are structured and ordered, predictable and safe. Unfortunately, in a large part, the Church has become program-oriented, which leaves many congregants feeling isolated and lonely, despite being part of a local church community.

Social media, on the other hand, is organic and alive - constantly growing and changing, as the lives of its participants are impacted by different social, cultural, justice, or political events. Ironically, it took the world to remind us how Jesus Himself did ministry. Take a quick read through the Gospels, and note how much of Jesus' ministry was organized and programmed. Not much. In fact, you might be surprised to learn that almost 100% of His ministry while on earth was based around interpersonal relationships - it was social in nature.

Jesus was (and is) highly social, and thus did most of His ministry around the dinner table, in the Temple, or down by the fishing boats. More profoundly still, is the fact that the entire purpose of the incarnation of Jesus was to mend the broken fellowship (aka relationship) between God and man. Both Jesus and the Father knew that man would never be able to remain sinless, and thus man could never enjoy a relationship with God. So, Jesus bridged that gap and came **all** the way for us. It's no wonder then that He ministered to the religious leaders in the temple, as well as to the sinners and tax collectors that wouldn't be caught dead in the temple. In His infinite grace and mercy, He did whatever He could to reach people on their turf and in the way that they were able to best receive His message of grace and love. The Apostle Paul echoes this idea of pervasive, invasive Christianity in 1 Corinthians when he writes:

[19] Though I am free and belong to no one, I have made myself a slave to everyone, to win as many as possible. [20] To the Jews I became like a Jew, to win the Jews. To those under the law I became like one under the law (though I myself am not under the law), so as to win those under the

law. ²¹ To those not having the law I became like one not having the law (though I am not free from God's law but am under Christ's law), so as to win those not having the law. ²² To the weak I became weak, to win the weak. I have become all things to all people so that by all possible means I might save some. ²³ I do all this for the sake of the Gospel, that I may share in its blessings.

-1 Corinthians 9:19-23 (NIV)

In essence, Paul is saying that there is nothing more important than the Gospel of salvation and getting it out to as many people as possible. There were no limits to Paul's unwavering dedication to presenting a clear Gospel to everyone he encountered. Centuries later, the Moravian missionaries laid hold of Paul's passion for evangelism and were known for selling themselves into slavery that they might win many for the kingdom. Fortunately, we're not asking you to sell yourself into literal slavery, but we would like you to consider how far you are willing to go for the sake of the Gospel. What does that look like in your digital life, and how do you reach people in a meaningful way through social media?

Banner blindness

Let's back up for a minute. If you've never heard the term "banner blindness", it's probably because it's a term developed by Internet advertisers to describe how people have learned to ignore the banners and advertisements that often appear on websites. It's like anything else that clutters our world - we tune out the noise. When the first billboard went up along the first highway it was probably quite noticeable for motorists. Now, with dozens of billboards along every mile of highway in the United States, most of us don't even consciously register the information being flashed at us as we whiz by. Why does this matter to you? Because banner blindness applies directly to how you engage the world via social media.

If the only things you ever post online are Bible verses to convince people to get saved (program oriented), then you'll get tuned out just as quickly as the ads that pop

> In order to effectively reach people, we need to return to the way that Jesus demonstrated.

up along the right edge of Facebook. In order to effectively reach people, we need to return to the way that Jesus demonstrated. We need to be deeply personal as well as relational. This starts by letting down our walls and by engaging people of the world in a genuine and personal way. You can begin by finding something you have in common, and begin to dialogue about that subject, from music to hobbies. Everything is within the limits of possibility. Once you begin to develop a relationship with them, they'll be more receptive to hearing the Gospel because you're now a friend sharing your personal experience with God rather than a religion salesman trying to make another sale.

Does this simple methodology really work? It absolutely does, since people use social media because they want to be social and fill the voids and areas that are lacking in their "real" lives.

The question that often comes up when talking with people about how Christians can use social media is, "What should I share online?" My response to this question is always the same, "What is actually worth sharing?" Facebook is piled high with garbage about "wars and rumors of wars". Twitter is cluttered with advertisements and self-promotion, most of which are not worth sharing. As Christians, we have been entrusted with a message that is worth sharing, and by and large, we don't share it. That's not to say that it is wrong to discuss the score of the latest game. It is, after all, **social** media. But turning into a Scripture posting tour-du-force doesn't work either, as it's the fastest way I know to get ignored. Jesus had neither Facebook nor Twitter, but as we study the impact and perceptions of social media, an interesting question emerges.

WWJT?

What would Jesus tweet? If Jesus were on the earth in bodily form today, would He use social media? Any answer we may come up with is speculation at best. What we can do, however, is look at the life of Christ, and the models and character He demonstrated in His lifetime to extrapolate an answer. It's a lot like the WWJD bracelets from the mid 1990's. We don't really know the answer, but we can make a good guess since we have been given the His Word, as well as the Holy Spirit who has promised to "guide us into all truth"[9]. Here's what we know. Jesus made an effort to go wherever people were. He spoke casually and relationally and often used venues outside the temple to preach. He turned every conversation into a teachable moment. And he spoke in a language that the uneducated, even children, could understand. So, if Jesus were alive today, would He be logged in? He used the dinner table didn't He? What is so different about social media? With roughly 50% of the world's population under

---

[9] John 16:13 (NKJV)

the age of thirty,[10] it comes as no surprise that social media is the language of this generation and of those to come. Even adults in their 50's and even 60's are signing up to join social media websites in droves. Social media is here to stay, and as Christians, we have the opportunity to engage the world through it. We should go out to where the people are, and make disciples of all nations. What other way can you name where you can literally reach all the nations of the world? In one place you have people and representatives from every tongue and nation online, on the same website at the same time. It has literally never been easier to engage the entire world at once.

We now live in a text-based world where words appear to be the primary form of communication. But words are not what people are really reading; they are reading our lives! They want to see how we treat others: how we love those around us. Jesus said,

---

[10] Erik Qualman / *April 13, 2010* Copyright © 2012 Socialnomicshttp://www.socialnomics.net/2010/04/13/over-50-of-the-worlds-population-is-under-30-social-media-on-the-rise/

"By this all men will know that you are my disciples, if you love one another."

- John 13:35 (NIV)

People want to see that love. In a desperate and hurting world, people want to see the bright and shining hope of the future.

I want to encourage you to think about what you want to say before you type it out. Ask the Holy Spirit to lead and guide you - He will. Ask yourself if what you are about to say points back to Jesus and His work in your life. If it does, then post away. To use the analogy of an advancing army, we're pushing into enemy territory rather than waiting for the enemy to approach us. Social media is the battleground for our time and for our words. For all of the distractions that social media presents, it also presents the remarkable opportunity to release the greatest message that the world has ever known in unfathomable lengths: the Gospel of Jesus Christ.

There's something amazing that happens when people hear the Gospel for the first time and realize their own sinful state. They realize that they have no hope of salvation except in Christ Jesus. And then something amazing happens.

I recently saw a woman come to Christ, and I watched overnight as she changed from a mess into a beautiful picture of what Jesus can do with each and every one of us. About a week after her salvation, I had a conversation with her in which she informed me that, as far as she could tell, the only reason that people aren't saved is because they have never been told. She believed so sincerely that if people only knew, they would believe.

Many of us seem to have forgotten the radical change that occurred in our own lives as a result of salvation, and so we add to the already cluttered cloudscape, rather than find a genuine, relational, and personal way to share Christ.

Friends and Followers

The six degrees of separation are narrowing. We have more "friends" than ever, but fewer close relationships. While social media has allowed us to expand our boundaries in terms of staying in touch with people in greater numbers, studies like the one recently conducted at Cornell University,[11] suggest that this generation has fewer close, intimate friends than the previous generation. And it's not due to our unwillingness to share personal information either. In fact, I believe that we are far too willing to share every detail of our daily lives with far too many people without consideration. But it seems that there

---

[11] "More Facebook Friends, Fewer Real Ones, Says Cornell Study" by Ned Potter
Nov. 8, 2011 / www.abcnews.go.com/Technology/facebook-friends-fewer-close-friends-cornell-sociologist/story?id=14896994#.TsZ9S2AuOPA

is a hidden benefit to flippant and careless transparency. Let me explain.

In the extreme circumstance that someone takes their own life or commits a serious crime, often times those closest to the person failed to see "the signs". While this is a sad reality, with social media there exists the opportunity for hundreds of people to notice the signs that a person in distress. The often transparent way that people post and share their feelings, opinions, moods, anger, and daily lives in general, now presents the possibility and also the responsibility for all of us to truly "see" people.

Step back in time with me to when Jesus walked the earth. Daily, it seems, as He traveled from place to place crowds would hear of His coming and flock to Him with their sick and afflicted- and Jesus healing them all[12]. As the sick were brought one by one and laid at Jesus' feet, the crowd, seeing the afflicted person's external need (blindness, leprosy, lame), would look on with bated breath wondering, "Will He be able to heal them?" He was able,

---

[12] Matthew 12:15, Luke 6:19

and He did, consistently. In fact Jesus always did more than just heal the obvious need. Instead, He always seemed to cut straight to people's hearts, healing years of rejection and loneliness, ultimately, forgiving their sin. In short, He made them whole. To heal the leprosy, for example, is to heal what others can see and to change that person's life from that moment forward - which in and of itself is wonderful. To be made whole, however, means that Jesus also healed the rejection, loneliness, bitterness, jealousy, and sense of abandonment that may have gone back many years as a result of the leprosy. Jesus was able to see people for who they really were and look beyond their carefully calculated game faces. I say this to challenge you and call you up to the same high standard that Jesus lived by. Of course, it's impossible for you to achieve this standard on your own, so ask the Holy Spirit to read between the lines of people's posts in social media with spiritual wisdom and discernment. He freely gives to all who ask.

Up to this point, we've mostly talked about your contribution to Internet-land. But what's equally important, is to know how to appropriately handle what others put out there. I encourage you to resist the urge to ignore someone's posts because "they're always so negative". Instead go the extra mile and really reach them! Social media is the top level where people will often drop their guard and say what they really feel without realizing that someone might read deeply into it. If these people are your "friends," then take on the role of friend and reach out to them in a personal and meaningful way. Let's get practical for a minute. "Hey, I've been noticing your posts lately. Are you OK? Is there anything I can do or pray with you about? When would be a good time we could talk?"

See that? It only took me about ten seconds to type that out. That's how long it takes to go from being a Facebook friend to being a **real** friend.

When you do this, its important to be aware of what you share publicly as this does present the issue of privacy. If you do reach out, and I hope that you do, please consider the other person's feelings and converse with them privately. While well intentioned, posting their business publicly can actually cause more hurt by causing them to feel put out or exposed. In social media, this translates into a private message, email, or text. Personal is better, so going out of your way to make a phone call or set up a face-to-face meeting is the best option and will often yield the best results. You have no idea how this choice may be the very thing that comes to someone's rescue. While a person may have 700 social media friends, you may be the only one who really sees that they're hurting and addresses their cry for help.

The 18 and under generation has grown up with social media, reality television, and YouTube, and therefore has an unusual need to be seen. While this level of openness and transparency can be used constructively in ways like we have just covered, there are dangers if common sense and basic social etiquette are naively ignored. For example, teenagers who willingly share their every move and location with an Internet audience fail to recognize the safety concerns that arise out of this pandemic trend. Many of these participants would most likely object to such accusations with, "I know the people I'm connected with."

...Really?

Social media gives us endless possibilities to be associated with an increasing number of groups and causes with a single click. It seems like just about every band, author, business, and non-profit on the planet has a Facebook page, and are constantly pumping content out into your network. That page for that band, that funny photo, that slogan you clicked "like" on...do you have any idea who is behind that page? Do you have any idea who now has access into the details of the lives of tens of thousands including yourself? Who now has access to your whereabouts?

What we're finding is that although people are more connected than at any other point in history, there also exists the possibility of being more exposed, entertained, and perhaps more lonely than ever.

Jesus said, "follow me" ...and somehow I don't think he meant on Twitter. The call He put out to the original twelve (as well as believers today) was for the sake of intimacy through proximity. The idea of the web is that we are all connected, and social media has proven that we are. But being connected (proximity) doesn't necessarily equate to intimacy. This connectedness creates a false sense of security and gives the illusion of intimacy, when intimacy is the very thing lacking from most 21st century relationships.

    Step back with me into the role of biblical disciple. When Jesus said, "follow me," what he meant, and what Jewish hearers would have understood, is "come with me and spend every waking and sleeping moment by my side until you are educated in all my ways". To be a disciple in Jewish culture was considered the highest honor and gave the disciple an all access pass into the teacher's life - everything is shared, and nothing is hidden.

As I think about the difference between a "friend" and a **friend,** the vast gap between the two becomes apparent. At the time of this writing, I (Bryce) had over 700 friends on Facebook. Yet, when I recently encountered a time of trouble, I found that there were very few people truly available for me to reach out to. I found myself in a paradoxical situation in that while the number of people I know is constantly expanding, the number of my true, close friends is diminishing. This makes perfect sense. Friendships are developed through spending time together, participating in various activities. But when the number of people you're friends with continues to grow, the amount of time you can invest in each individual friend decreases.

True friendship is defined by intimacy, or to be cliché, 'in-to-me-see'. But honestly, it's only a cliché because it has been tested and tried through the years, and has been found true. If the level of your friendships is based upon keeping up with people via their latest tweets, then it begs the question "are you friends at all"?

Redefining friends

Let me be the first to say that the number of friends you have online means nothing. I (still Bryce) was in college when Facebook was first introduced and remember the frenzy that swept my college, as students everywhere raced to reconnect with high school classmates, as well as every new person they met. It was a popularity contest of which I was a participant. And I too raced to "friend" every person from every class, and virtually everyone I met in the elevator, laundry room, or at the gym (the one time I went). After four years and hundreds of Internet connections later, I arrived at the startling realization that I didn't really connect with any of them. For years I had a long list of friends that I didn't know at all, and they didn't know me. At first, some might wish me a happy birthday at Facebook's prompting, and others would sometimes respond to uncharacteristically clever status updates. With time, however, the number of coveted 'likes' under each new status update would suffer and eventually, even those once great laundry-room acquaintances would quietly un-friend me. It was then that I realized that I was still performing for people's approval. Social media was a giant, global popularity contest and I was trying desperately to compete.

I'd like to reiterate that social media itself is not evil and we should take care to not throw the baby out with the bath water just because it tends to be a swamp of shallow, 'me'-centric relationships.... Wow, when I say it like that, social media sounds like a horrible place and not like the powerful and helpful tool that it really is! But fret not, my bewildered reader; complicated times merit simple solutions.

When It Matters

It's easy to forget the reach that social media has. For just a moment, I want you to picture a late night radio talk show personality as he burns the midnight oil. He sits alone in a small studio - just him alone with a microphone, four walls, and his thoughts to keep him company. He might feel isolated and alone in his sound booth, but in that same moment his words are reaching the ears of thousands, even millions of listeners if his show is syndicated. So, while he sits alone in a small room with a microphone, the impact of his words is immeasurably large as his words touch people as they travel through life. Wherever his listeners may be, whether in their car, in a coffee shop, in their home, or at work, he is engaging them directly. It is his understanding of the influence he has that governs what he does and says while on the air. No matter how alone he feels sitting in that small studio, he knows that his words are not bound by the four walls that surround him. Since he has such a far-reaching platform, laws imposed on him by the Federal Communication Commission, as well as his radio station's company restrictions, social pressure from his listeners, and his own personal boundaries, all play a role in what he says and how he says it. The fact is the DJ is ultimately responsible for every word that he speaks while on the air.

Social media works in the same way, except this time, you are the DJ. You may feel, when you log in to update your status, like it's just you, your computer, and your feelings. But your words have a much further reach and impact than you may realize. Through social media, your words are like those of the radio talk show host, in that they are indiscriminately broadcast in all directions, and contain the potential to reach many people. And while the words of a radio host are live and fleeting, your words typed in social media can have a very long shelf life. This leaves a lot of opportunity for good, as well as plenty of room to do some damage as well.

As a parent, I (Chuck) teach my kids that when it's important, when it matters, don't post or text. I know...I know...we said this wasn't going to be a rules and regulations book - and it wont' be. But we never promised that we wouldn't bury a few suggestions we've learned the hard way deep into chapter 7. We actually feel that we would be doing you a great disservice if we toss around concepts and ideas and then fail to get down to a practical level.

Notice we didn't make this the first chapter? It's likely that if you've gotten this far you're willing to move from surface level ideas and concepts into some of the different ways our personal faiths and social media can truly intertwine. Some things just need to be said - some practical advice if you will. You might be thinking, "OK, now they're pushing me out of my comfort zone," and maybe we are, but mostly we're just sharing our experiences (the successes as well as the mistakes). You have the benefit of learning from them without having to clean up some of the messes yourself. So, buckle up for a few minutes. It's time to get real.

When You Are At Odds With Someone

Listen, when it matters…when it's important…talk to the person. It's not just good Internet practice, it's the Scriptural thing to do. Texting, for example, should never be the method of choice to resolve conflict or express strong feelings or emotions. In general, half sentences and abbreviated words via a text do not provide the context, emotion, clarity, or engagement necessary to fully resolve a situation. Even the words "I'm sorry" in a text, however sincere, do not carry the same depth of meaning as they do when you are looking someone in the eyes. In the same way, public posts through social media should never be considered a valid or reasonable means of achieving conflict resolution. This includes, dare I say, vague, passive-aggressive posts (or posts disguised as Scriptures) aimed at your offender. Just because you don't name the person directly doesn't make the method any more appropriate or wise. Chances are good that the person you're aiming at will know that you're talking about them even if you don't use their name. There's a big difference between posting a Scripture and sending someone a "message."

"Moreover if your brother sins against you, go and tell him his fault between you and him alone. If he hears you, you have gained your brother."

- Matthew 18:15 (NKJV)

Jesus is encouraging face to face confrontation. For the sake of love, go to your brother and work it out with him directly, no matter how difficult this may be. Many people believe that to be unified as the body of Christ we can't have disagreements among us. But since the Church is made up of fallible human beings, disagreements, contentions, and offenses are bound to occur. When they do, it is our responsibility to search out a method of resolve that provides the opportunity for clarity and long lasting healing. Jesus' mandate in this verse will never be adequately replaced by any form of technology.

This is the method Jesus instructs us to use when we have an issue with someone, and I firmly believe that

2,000 years later it is still the best method afloat. Technology can't manage to replace this mandate- although its use as a replacement does tend to confuse the issues and make matters worse. When it truly matters, lay technology aside. It becomes a heart issue. If you really wish to resolve an issue with someone, then go to them. In my life I've seen too many bridges burned in cases that were completely resolvable had those involved talked it out instead of texting, or spoken instead of posted.

Life changing events

Recently I (Chuck) was at the hospital with a family who had just lost a family member. Within the same hour of the departed's passing, while we were still at the hospital, posts began to surface on Facebook. The messages appeared to be well-intentioned condolences which appeared to be genuine. But in the abbreviated timeframe of the tragedy's unfolding there were immediate family members who had yet to be notified. Can you imagine inadvertently discovering the news of a family member's death through a social media post? Sadly, I've seen this more than once already. It was actually a situation like the one described that led us to seriously consider the need for a book addressing appropriate usage of social media.

Let me make a suggestion here. When there has been a passing or tragedy of some sort, use restraint and don't post anything until there has been a sufficient window of time for the family to contact those who should receive the news properly. Family and close friends should not receive tragic news from an outsider via social media. It is vital that we resist the urge to react in a "knee-jerk" fashion and post, even in sincerity, but without consideration for the family, extended relatives and close friends. Let me make a suggestion that perhaps you can use as a personal guideline. When someone passes, if you are not an immediate family member with the authority to make such information public, just wait, exercise discernment, and use the knowledge of what you know to pray for the family.

"The prayer of a righteous man is powerful and effective"
- James 5:16 (NIV)

After you've seen something posted by the bereaved family then go ahead an offer your condolences. If you can, make a phone call since it's more personal. Someone will always post right away with the best of intentions, though they haven't thought through the situation. Other's will post, and some love to be the bearer of news. That doesn't necessarily give you the green light. But do your best to avoid the pressure to join in and remember that there's no hurry. Which begs the question, "Do I have the right to be the one to make private news public?" Here's where listening to the Holy Spirit comes in by asking yourself, "Am I posting because I feel led to? Or do I have a genuine concern for the people involved? Am I seeking the recognition that comes from being the first to know?" Even if others are posting…wait. Be sensitive. And if you see others posting before it's appropriate, find a way to teach them about the importance of sensitivity and protocol. But do it through a private message and in love. It's a matter of honor, etiquette, and decency, people will probably respond well to if it is presented to them in a loving way. As the Body of Christ, this is an area where we can certainly set the bar higher, and be a living example of discernment and sensitivity.

Sympathy Cards and Me-Monsters

"Does anyone see me? ...Does anyone care?" This would be the literal translation of a lot of posts in social media if we took the time to read between the lines. This underlying need to be noticed is especially popular amongst the teenage crowd, but users of all ages regularly employ this attention-getting method. I'm sure we've all seen it, and many of us have done it: a vague post that appears to have been carefully designed to elicit the response of others.

It seems that when people post in a way that is designed to get a response such as in the example above, they aren't really expecting anyone to fix an issue with a tweet or Facebook post. Rather, there is an underlying need to know that someone is there. Likewise, they want to be assured that someone out there in the vast reaches of cyberspace cares enough about them to notice. This is a need that reaches to the fundamental core of every human. Each and every one of us wants to know the same thing - that we are worthy of love.

If you notice someone on your "friends" list is regularly posting in a way that seems to be seeking responses, sympathy, or compliments, I encourage you to take the time to read between the lines. There is a clear deficit in their life, and God might use you to meet that need and bring life-changing healing. Even if you're tired or a little frustrated about all their complaining, resist the urge to write that individual off and ignore their posts. You may even catch yourself thinking, "he/she is always so negative! All they ever want is to be the focus of everyone's attention. They're such a me-monster!" This line of thinking may be spot on. But what should we do about it?

As a side note: If you realized after reading that last section that we just described your behavior in social media, I want to remind you that you have the opportunity to ask the Holy Spirit to be the one to meet that need rather than trying to seek to fill it yourself. There is no shame in being needy and coming to Him with your hurts and problems. In fact, He built us in that way for a purpose so that we would rely on Him to meet all our needs! He is a good Abba (which just means "Daddy") who loves to provide for His children. *"My God shall provide all my needs according to His riches in glory"*[13]. I guarantee that when you ask Him, He will fill up your heart to overflowing, and when He does, you get to pour out that love to all the other me-monsters out there in the world. After all, God might use you to meet the needs of others. Besides, isn't it more satisfying when affirming compliments come to you unsolicited anyway?

One of my favorite stories in Scripture is that of the woman who had been healed of a longstanding illness. Here is the passage from the 25th chapter from the Gospel of Mark in the Message Translation.

---

[13] Philippians 4:19

²⁵⁻²⁹ A woman who had suffered a condition of hemorrhaging for twelve years—a long succession of physicians had treated her, and treated her badly, taking all her money and leaving her worse off than before—had heard about Jesus. She slipped in from behind and touched his robe. She was thinking to herself, "If I can put a finger on his robe, I can get well." The moment she did it, the flow of blood dried up. She could feel the change and knew her plague was over and done with.

³⁰ At the same moment, Jesus felt energy discharging from him. He turned around to the crowd and asked, "Who touched my robe?"

³¹ His disciples said, "What are you talking about? With this crowd pushing and jostling you, you're asking, 'Who touched me?' Dozens have touched you!"

³²⁻³³ But he went on asking, looking around to see who had done it. The woman, knowing what had happened, knowing she was the one, stepped up in fear and trembling, knelt before him, and gave him the whole story.

³⁴ Jesus said to her, "Daughter, you took a risk of faith, and now you're healed and whole. Live well, live blessed! Be healed of your plague."

- Mark 25:25-34 (The Message)

My favorite part of the story comes in verse 33 when she "gave Him the whole story". What a profound picture! Here He is, the King of Glory, on His way through a crowd of people who are clamoring for His attention, and one woman touches the hem of His robe. When she comes forward the Scripture tells us that she tells him the "whole story" - which according to the book of Matthew began twelve years prior[14]. That's a long story! Despite what was going on around Him or his prior plans, I suspect Jesus listened to the whole story because He knew that being heard and accepted was an important step in her healing.

No one sets out to be a me-monster, and I would bet that most people who are, despise that part of themselves. The fact is that people are only me-monsters because of the

---

[14] Matt 9:20-22

hurts and pains that life has caused them. Many of them have never felt valued by others, and thus lack a healthy dose of self-appreciation and have difficulty receiving love from the Father. They may not have the self-confidence required to look beyond themselves and their own situations, so they try to get ahead by self-promoting. When people post in a way that seeks reaction it's probably because they need one. So, when you encounter these people, do what Jesus did- look past their obvious pain and listen to the whole story.

Maybe you just finished this section and realized, "Wow, I guess that's me…I do that all the time." Then ask yourself honestly what it is that you are lacking in real relationships that you are hoping virtual comments might fill. Pray and ask God to heal up any past hurts and fill that void with Himself. First and

> When people post in a way that seeks reaction, it's likely because they need one.

foremost, seek a deeper relationship with Him. Then focus on developing a handful of key relationships in a more meaningful way in your own life. A recent study conducted by the Greater Good Science Center found that one of the indisputable keys to happiness is having a few good friends - or quality over quantity as they put it[15]. Having 1,000 connections in social media is great, but having 5 real, close, and accountable relationships in the Body of Christ hold far greater value, and produce the tangible fruit of happiness in your life.

OMG!

Young people, let's be honest. Social media abbreviations are a quick and convenient way to say something without typing out all of the words. I get it. From "BF" (best friend), to "TTYL" (talk to you later), to the ever-popular "LOL" (laughing out loud), there is a long list of shortcuts that have become part of the fabric of our online vocabulary. Don't misunderstand me, as long as the

---

[15] https://fbcdn-sphotos-a.akamaihd.net/hphotos-ak-snc7/428730_3023699043177_1583769351_2531154_1434821410_n.jpg

reader understands what you're trying to say through abbreviations, it's a great way to communicate and illustrate, all at the same time. There is a visual difference between "LOL" (laughing out loud) and "ROFL" (rolling on the floor laughing).

But then there's the trend of abbreviating profanity within this new way of communicating. Some of us are getting numb to its use as if to say, "Well, it's not like I'm really cussing." I really want you to give this some thought and prayer. Using social media abbreviations that imply profanity IS the same thing as using the profanity itself. Maybe you don't us the "F" word in your spoken vocabulary, but is it really all right to use the letter "F" in an abbreviated phrase to imply it? What about other letters or symbols that mean or represent inappropriate language for that matter? It seems that this generation has adopted the view that using abbreviations somehow gives license to ramification-free cussing.

When I as the reader see your abbreviated expletive, I don't read the letter, I read it as the word it represents. Perhaps you've gotten into the habit of using abbreviated expletives and figure it's no big deal. But I want you to pray about it and consider a higher standard. Don't allow yourself to become numb and live in the shallow end of the social media pool. Raise the standard of speech for your generation. You may not think that anyone will notice that you no longer use abbreviated expletives- and maybe they won't. But something doesn't have to be noticed or acknowledged in order for it to be the right thing to do. Look at this way. As a Believer, should you really be implying language you wouldn't use at the dinner table? Let's call it what it is and move on. We want to honor God with our words and our communications, and it's not fair to the reader for you to impose profanity on them under the guise of abbreviation. Did you know the word profanity comes from the Latin meaning "outside the Temple"? Marinate on that for a second if you need to. Social media may make it easy to compartmentalize your social life, but I want to challenge you to be the best you can be in every realm of life - including the "you" behind your fancy, high-tech screen.

"Do not let any unwholesome talk come out of your mouths, but only what is helpful for building others up according to their needs, that it may benefit those who listen."

- Ephesians 4:29 (NIV)

Abbreviations do not count as loopholes. Let's raise the bar, shall we? Let's move on.

Rise of the Thumb Tribe

When the first European explorers first encountered the indigenous African peoples in the obscure regions of Africa, they no doubt wondered at how these people managed to live. They didn't observe European customs or traditions nor did they live with many of the material possessions the Europeans would have been accustomed to. Not only that, but their methodology and techniques for daily living would have been different as well. How strange farming with a stick must look when you're used to a plow.

On the other hand, I suppose it's safe to say that the indigenous Africans probably thought the same of their European visitors. The Africans ate simply and lived off the land while the settlers would have packaged, barreled, and cured products. The two groups stood scratching their heads as they watched how the other went about doing things. The above examples are what are known as culture shock.

As anyone who has ever spent an extended time in another country will tell you, culture shock still happens today. I (Bryce) grew up in Qatar, a tiny Arab nation in the Middle East. If you're looking at a map, it's the thumb that sticks off Saudi Arabia into the Persian Gulf. My family moved there in 1991, right after Desert storm. I was six at the time. Being a child, I didn't really experience culture shock because I had lived overseas since the day I was born: Kuwait first, then Pakistan, and then Qatar. But I was an American and I knew it; And so did everyone else. In a land of dark and beautiful people my skin was a constant reminder of my origins - not to mention the fact that my Arabic was terrible.

I didn't actually experience culture shock until I was fifteen years old, when my family moved home to the United States. All of the sudden, I was a stranger in an unfamiliar land, and I didn't know what to do with myself. I didn't know the slang, understand most jokes, or get references to movies or pop culture. I simply couldn't understand why women wore their underwear (bikinis) to the beach when the traditional dress for an Arab woman seldom showed the ankles! I thought Eddie Bauer was the most popular boy in school, and I was always puzzled when people asked me what state Qatar was in. I was still an American, at least according to my passport, but culturally I couldn't have been further removed.

So what is culture anyway? Culture is a fluid list of all the things we share in common that help us relate to one another. It might include language, geography, ideologies, religion, diet, clothing, industry, hobbies, weather, or any number of specific items shared amongst a community. It's the things that we all have in common that make up our collective identity.

When we get saved, we automatically become part of another smaller culture, or a subculture, called Christianity. Words like "sanctification" and "redemption" become part of our vocabulary, and are understood within most Christian circles. Step outside that circle, and ask the girl who sits next to you in math class how her sanctification is coming along, and watch as a puzzled expression distorts her normally proportioned face. She's not part of the club (not to mention that it's kind of an odd question to begin with).

Culture is important because it serves as a set of unspoken rules and social codes that determines who is accepted in a particular group and also outlines what constitutes acceptable behavior within that group. So, why should the Internet be any different? Several years ago in Japan, people began to classify those who are chronically on their mobile devices as members of the 'thumb tribe' (in reference to texting specifically). We have chosen to use the term **cloud culture** to refer to the current and future landscape of social media as a whole, as well as to describe the attitudes and behaviors of those who actively participate in it.

Join the Conversation

Did you know, that the phrase Twitter uses to encourage you to sign up for their service is "join the conversation?" It's quite profound how they've managed to sum this whole book up in three words (now is a good time to see if you saved the receipt from this purchase). Social media is a conversation. It's the back and forth, organic, evolving dialog of the people of the world. And it doesn't stop when you log off.

I'm constantly amazed how the Genesis account tells us that God walked with Adam in the cool of the day right before God drops a bomb and says...

"It is not good for the man to be alone"
- Genesis 2:18 (NIV)

What? God said this? How could the great All in All say this? If there was ever a time to wonder inquisitively at the complexity of God, this might be the time. Was Adam's being with God the same as being alone? Of course not! We know what he meant; man needs peer-to-peer companionship. So God caused man to fall into a deep sleep and removed a rib from man and proceeded to fashion woman from the rib. I should be honest with you and tell you that I have no idea what this looked like or how long it took, but it seems clear that woman was formed and crafted which seems to imply some time.

There are two things which are clear from this passage. First is that we were created to be social in nature, not unlike meerkats or pigeons. Second, and maybe more significant at this point in human history, relationships require time and crafting.

The Bravery of Friendship.

It's so easy to click "accept" to a friend request on Facebook even if we've never met the person on the other end of the line. But developing real friendships is difficult, as it requires a certain amount of intimacy and commitment to the other person.

When my wife and I (Bryce) were dating, I was careful to show her only the parts of myself that I was proud of - the parts that were attractive and easy to love. Once we were married and moved in together, something changed. Suddenly, it was impossible to hide my bad habits and emotional woundedness and for the first time, my wife was able to get to know who I really was.

Thankfully, in spite of my shortcomings, we're still married. And happily I might add. In fact, the simple fact that she knows all of my weaknesses grants me freedom to grow, change, and learn to be the best me possible. But it was certainly a battle to get to that point and it wouldn't have been possible without commitment.

Commitment is of maximum importance when talking about any kind of relationship, because without it you'll end up with superficial acquaintances - similar in most respects to Facebook friends. On the other hand, when commitment exists between friends, then just like in the example with my wife, you and your friends are free to be yourselves.

Tearing Down Digital Walls

To a certain extent, social media is the wall we hide behind. It's a way that we can satisfy our need for human interaction while at the same time keeping people out of the deep places of our lives. Through social media we are able to control our relationships to ensure that we don't get hurt. After all, the people closest to you are the ones with the most power to hurt you. So, limit how close they can get, and you effectively limit their ability to hurt you.

...social media is the wall we hide behind.

On the flip side, the extent to which we limit people's ability to hurt us inadvertently limits their ability to love us, and also our ability to receive that love and love them back. As Christians we are called to be extravagant lovers - not bound by fear or limitation - imitating our namesake, Jesus. It is impossible to love extravagantly when you're hiding behind walls and trying to protect yourself with crossed arms. For this reason, the Lord has promised to go before us and fight for us[16]; He is our strong tower - He is our

---

[16] Isaiah 52:12, Deuteronomy 3:22

protector. Let's do our best to get out of the way and choose to be vulnerable, allowing Him to do His job.

I love social media as much as anyone else. Just today, I was able to connect with a childhood friend that I had lost touch with a decade ago, and that wouldn't have been possible without Facebook. I found out that she spent a year doing missions work in Africa and now is traveling through South America with a team of radicals preaching the Gospel in every village they go to. The team is also documenting their journey and sharing testimonies via Facebook; some of which are going viral and are encouraging Christians all over the world! And it's only because of Facebook that I know about any of it! On the personal level my friend and I have been able to catch up on the past decade and rekindle our childhood friendship. So, there are monumental benefits to this inter web, but ask yourself this question. "Am I using social media as a wall to keep people out of the deep places in my life? or am I developing real, deep, face to face relationships with the people in my circle".

God's Goal - Relationships

It seems unlikely that a conversation about social media in the 21st century would end up in the book of Genesis. Then again, it seems almost fitting. In the ever-evolving saga of human history, when technology, philosophy, and innovation come at us faster than most of us can manage, we need a constant- we need truth. In this case, the account of creation in Genesis shines exactly the light that we need.

In the beginning...

With the opening of Genesis 1, we watch the Invisible Uncreated create the physical and visible universe in which we now live. Through the writings of Moses we are given a front row seat to the most spectacular performance in history. We can't see it yet, but somehow we can sense that there is movement on the stage (vs. 2). The lights come up (vs. 3) and for the first time in creation, a void and formless earth emerges on the stage of history. With a word from the Master Conductor, land springs up (vs. 9) from the water and appears on the earth (vs. 10). Then, right on cue, grass appears on the land and the once void earth is populated by the Uncreated until it teems with life (vs. 24). But the best is yet to come. As every performer knows, it is best to hold the audience in suspense until you reveal the final act and grand finale. So in the beginning, the Uncreated creates His masterpiece- you.

While the majesty of the Genesis could be (and has filled) whole volumes of books to describe the creation story, we're only interested in one verse.

"Then God said, "Let Us make man in Our image, according to Our likeness;"

- Genesis 1:26 (NKJV)

Now if you're anything like me, you just pictured a little lump of flesh-colored clay sprouting arms and legs, as a man with a long white beard and fatherly smile watches over to make sure that it turns out all right. Contextually this is completely incorrect but still paints an amusing picture. According to the Scriptures, when we arrive at this verse, we only know three things about God.

> **1.) God is a creator**
> **2.) God has dominion over the whole earth**
> **3.) There is an "us" involved**

In my humble and non-scholarly opinion, the third is by far the most interesting of the three. God, in His infinite wisdom and unlimited ability, decided to create man just as He is - with a need for interaction, unity, and us. It's not a stretch to say that you were created with the innate need to know people and be known by people (and I don't mean being a celebrity). In fact, many of the celebrities I've worked with over the years are some of the loneliest people I've ever met.

How can this be, you may wonder to yourself, when everyone knows who they are? I think it's because many celebrities, due to their high profile and the constant demands that are placed on them, miss out on the basic need to be known personally and intimately. This is the reason why a celebrity can have all of the fame this world has to offer and yet be so dysfunctional privately.

If further proof is needed, a quick look at Jesus should be sufficient to quiet any remaining doubts. Jesus, being the Son of God, could have had it anyway He wanted. Rather than being born to Roman aristocracy, He chose to enter the world as a child to common people. His childhood would have been spent playing with his brothers and sisters while also learning to be a carpenter like his father Joseph. Fast forward a few years, and we see Jesus coming out of the river Jordan being led away into the desert to be tempted by the devil. This is one of the last times that we see Jesus alone in Scripture. After He called the twelve they were by His side day and night. Even when He wept in Gethsemane they were close by.

It's also important to note that Jesus picked the twelve. They weren't some sort of inheritance that He got stuck with. He chose them just like He chose you and me.

If nothing else, this alone demonstrates the relational nature of God. This desire for communion (aka relationships) is the same desire that was imparted to you at your creation and recorded in Genesis 1:26. *"Let us make man in **our** image..."*(NASB). We see then that the Glory of God is made famous and clearly displayed through relationships.

Not-so Smooth Operator

Social Media, as we've established, is neutral. It is neither good nor evil, and is simply a tool in your hand. How you choose to use it is up to you. When people rely on social media as the primary, or even sole basis for relationships, they come up short. And many people are suddenly finding that their lives feel surprisingly empty. Knowing a person involves more than a uni-dimensional knowing **about** them, which is what social media is designed to do - transmit information from one person to the next. To really know and to be known, we need to

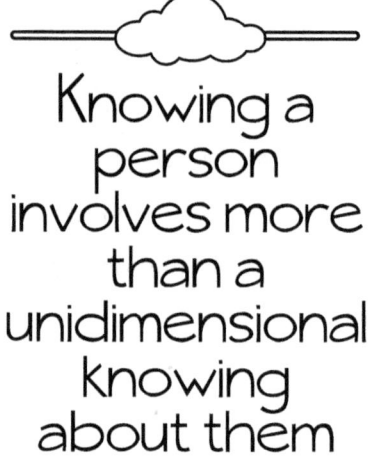

Knowing a person involves more than a unidimensional knowing about them

move beyond the screen in front of us.

The old adage is right. The eyes really are the window to the soul, and they are the original method of communication. With all that has changed in our post-modern world this simple truth has not- the eyes are still surprisingly good at conveying feeling.

Have you ever seen Blue Man Group? Week after week patrons flood Blue Man theaters to watch three guys in blue paint as they perform a hilarious and awe-inspiring 110 minute social commentary - all without saying a word. Much of the show's communication is conveyed through the expressions of the performers' eyes.

To further our point, your eyes will always tell the truth of what's going on inside even if your mouth happens to say something different. Smitten couples spend copious amounts of time just staring into each other's eyes, while old married couples can communicate volumes of affections across a crowded room with a single glance. The eyes may very well be the most sincere communicator of the inner life.

In the 21st century when we spend more time staring at a screen than looking at a person, we tend to lose track of our incredible ability to communicate non-verbally. When unfiltered non-verbal communication gives way to calculated bits of information via non-personal delivery methods something horrible happens. It's the quiet death of the human element. This tragedy often goes unnoticed due to its widespread social acceptance and because it's far easier to hide behind digital walls than to be honest and vulnerable with real people. In all of our self –protecting, we lose intimacy. Which begs the question, "Is it better to be safe when we no longer possess the very thing for which we were created?"

Whenever my wife and I (Bryce) hit a rough patch in our marriage, we (try to) make the intentional decision to do what we call "eye-gaze time". Even in those moments when steam is billowing out of our ears and we'd rather slug each other in the nose than have a civil conversation, we pause to look into each other's eyes. When we do this, the most amazing thing happens. All the anger we are feeling immediately evaporates, and we fall into each other's arms, usually laughing about how our gigantic fight was over something so petty and small. This cools us off and reminds us that we are both imperfect working towards perfection as God heals us up from past hurts. And ultimately it restores our humanity.

Jesus was infinitely intimate with everyone He encountered. He had nothing to hide and thus gave all of Himself to anyone who might receive Him. He then proverbially turns to us and invites us on a privileged journey of extreme vulnerability. In the Gospel of John, we're told that the world will know that we are Christians by our love (John 13:35), and love requires us to know and be known by one another.

We know what extravagant love is because we have a Savior who is relentless in His pursuit to demonstrate His love to us. The world is not so fortunate. Yet the idea that people need love and acceptance even echoes through the theories of secular psychologists and we were handed this truth thousands of years before Dr. Freud and Carl Jung 'discovered' this basic human need. But in an increasingly isolated world many people substitute one-night stands and empty meaningless flings for the love that they so desperately desire. They spiral into depression as their lives lose all remaining semblances of humanity, and they quietly die inside.

Unfortunately, many Christians find themselves in the same place. I know I've felt that way before but rejoice in the truth that I never have to feel that way again. God has already told us His plans for us; that we, as brothers and sisters in Christ, may be one as Jesus and the Father are one (John 17:21). As the Trinity was in the beginning, so are you and I to be now. And in doing so we become a light in the world: a thing of beauty that causes the inhabitants of the earth to take notice.

It's great that you're Facebook profile is up to date; mine is too. But let's make an effort to push through the virtual reality before us and into each other's real lives. Find someone and plan a face-to-face meeting. Go get a cup of coffee or grill hamburgers in the back yard - whatever you do, try to have more face time with real human beings. Learn to walk through life with friends and people who you can learn to love, and watch as God perfects His perfect love in you (1 John 4:12). I (Chuck) will never forget walking into our youth group at Church one Wednesday evening to find about a dozen teenagers sitting quietly…all looking at their cell phones. Each of them interacting with people they weren't physically with. No one was speaking to each other - yet their peers and friends right next to them in the same room!

So here's a challenge for you - find ways to use social media to build relationships in the real world. Log on with the intent of connecting face-to-face; go online to get off-line, and I promise that your life will increase in fulfillment and meaning.

So...Now What?!?

At the very core of social media is you - the user. After all, Facebook with no friends is pointless. Twitter with no followers is useless. Without the user, we revert back to the dawn of the Internet, a time when static web pages adorned the Internet like hand-me-down ornaments on a Christmas tree. The pages weren't interactive. Heck, they weren't even pretty. Rather they existed to display information, and that was it. When social media came along, the rules changed. Dynamic, interactive websites sprang up all over and the user was handed an invitation to help create the content that the website was to display. Forums, threads, blogs, and community pages started springing up everywhere as new users joined the movement en masse and the once dull Internet came alive. Where once websites displayed stoic information, now blank pages lay waiting to be shaped by a global community of connected users.

This is you, and me for that matter. We are participants in the greatest collaboration in human history. We have enlisted ourselves in the sprawling cyber community known as the "the web" and we are builders of the next great world. We have the opportunity to lay the foundation for the future of the Internet and create well and build that which will last. How will you do that?

In the end, if social media is ultimately about relationships, then the goal, first and foremost, should be to strengthen and deepen our relationship with God as well as the horizontal relationships in our lives. Social media, texting and the like have quickly become the fabric of our communications which, if we're not careful, can hijack our free time and inhibit the development of these meaningful relationships. But first things first; we need to understand that our chief relationship is with *Him* and then with one another. With this revelation in place His presence in our lives will permeate and govern our presence online. This is what will allow us to be conduits for His presence in the *Cloud Culture*.

"You Are Now Entering Your Mission Field"

These are the words that have adorned the walls at the exit doors of our church sanctuary for years. They serve not only as an ever-present reminder of our purpose, but also that our mission field is always within our grasp and all around us. We've brought you to this point with intention- not to cause you to question social media and whether it should have a role in the Christian life, or to alert you to the potential dangers that exist. Rather, this revolutionary time in history is a highway to mobilize you in your faith in a way that was never before possible.

To this point we've discussed ways that we can personally and individually hold a higher standard with our communications. But let's look now at the possibilities that we hold collectively…as a Body. It's time for a locker room pep talk. This isn't the time to step back or retreat, but instead to lunge forward and press in. This is our version of the monologue William Wallace gives to his troops in the movie "Braveheart". It's where we hope to impart to you the vision that we have in our hearts, and inspire you to greatness in His Kingdom. But first, let me start with a story.

It's Spring 2012, as I (Chuck) sit down to write this. I'm attempting to sum up the possibilities of social media and consider how we can bring this book to a close in a way that serves as a springboard rather than a conclusion when my two teenagers ask me again, "Dad, have you watched the video yet?". The video they were referring to is a social media campaign to bring attention to the atrocities committed by African warlord Joseph Kony. The irony is that while I'm racking my brain to find an appropriate and inspiring end to *Cloud Culture*, the best illustration in years was unfolding that same afternoon as 60 million people from around the world logged on to view a single YouTube video. In just a few hours, one murderous man became a household name thanks to the power of social media. The video went around the world in viral fashion as it bounced from person to person on every peer-to-peer sharing platform around.

To me, this confirms the significance of the book you hold in your hand. I'm encouraged that one video can reach 60 million plus people in a day. I'm excited that a single message can touch every nation on the earth in a matter of minutes. Which makes me wonder what other message can we send? For the first time in history, there exists the possibility for normal people - not celebrities or world leaders - to communicate globally. It no longer has to be imagined or exaggerated. In fact, it's reality already.

You are now entering your mission field. Where is that exactly? Chances are it's sitting on your desk or in your pocket already. You no longer have to travel to Africa to reach people in Africa. Likewise, you don't have to raise large amounts of money and block off weeks of time in order to enter the mission field. Can you see it yet? Do you realize the gift we have been handed with social media? It's time to paint with the broadest of brushes.

India as a nation may be far away from you, but her people are as close as your smart phone or your computer. Geographically, Africa may be an out of reach destination for you, but many of her people are as close as Twitter. With your smart phones and social media accesses, your mission field is literally in your hands 24/7 now. Every time you access social media via your phone or computer, you are now entering your mission field. You can simultaneously speak to close personal friends and people you've never met on the other side of the world with one push of a button. Now THAT is power at your fingertips.

> Every time you access social media… you are now entering your mission field.

"And He said to them, Go into all the world and preach the gospel to every creature."

- Mark 16:15 (NKJV)

Consider it done. You can 'go into all the world' from wherever you are right now. The game has changed in a big way, and with the right perspective, you can see that it has changed for the better. If one man's evil and murderous acts can be made famous in a day through social media, then just imagine what we can collectively do for the cause of Christ. Imagine if for every invitation to join Farmville there was an invitation to know the King of Glory. What if for every person who watched the latest trending video one a person became aware of the Living God. Can you imagine it? Can you catch this vision? What if we spread His fame throughout the earth using these inexpensive resources, which are already within our grasp every day? What we need is for the world to meet Jesus as a result of the natural outpouring of the deepening relationship that Christians have with the one true God. Imagine how that spillover into social media would absolutely change the world. ...Imagine!

Now stop imagining…and GO! No, really, go… into all the world. The mission field is no longer reserved only for those with a specific calling, or the time, or the resources to travel. Are there risks? Maybe a few. Just as there are risks present when we travel to minister to various nations and regions, there are risks that exist within social media as well. But don't let those risks smother the fire of the calling upon your life. There is a mandate on all of our lives and the access to it is as close as the tips of your fingers. The world is waiting, and watching your digital life. May you be the one to truly change the world as we know it.

Remember, you are His presence in the Cloud.

Additional copies of this book and subsequent titles from Seven Leaf Press are available on our website:

www.SevenLeafPress.com
and
www.CloudCultureBook.com

as well as online book sellers everywhere.

www.ingramcontent.com/pod-product-compliance
Lightning Source LLC
Chambersburg PA
CBHW060834050426
42453CB00008B/693